Birds up close

# Rainforest Birds

A Bobbie Kalman Book

Crabtree Publishing Company

# Birds up close
## A Bobbie Kalman Book

### For Petrina,
### a really colorful bird

**Editor-in-Chief**
Bobbie Kalman

**Writing team**
Bobbie Kalman
Jacqueline Langille
Niki Walker

**Text research**
Jacqueline Langille
Tara Harte
April Fast

**Managing editor**
Lynda Hale

**Series editor**
Niki Walker

**Editor**
Greg Nickles

**Photo research**
Jacqueline Langille

**Computer design**
Lynda Hale
Andy Gecse (cover concept)

**Special thanks to**
Doug Wechsler, Academy of Natural Sciences, Philadelphia, PA
Ron Rohrbaugh, Cornell Laboratory of Ornithology

**Production coordinator**
Hannelore Sotzek

**Photographs**
Jim Bryant: page 30
Russell C. Hansen: page 12
James Kamstra: cover, pages 5, 7 (bottom), 9, 10 (bottom), 17
Tom McHugh/The National Audubon Society Collection/Photo Researchers:
    pages 18, 23 (top right)
Tom Stack & Associates: John Cancalosi: page 24; Warren & Genny Garst:
    page 16; Chip & Jill Isenhart: page 31; Brian Parker: page 27; Larry Tackett:
    page 11; Roy Toft: page 15
Y. R. Tymstra: page 28
Valan Photos: John Cancalosi: pages 19 (bottom), 25 (bottom left), 29;
    Ken Cole: page 8; Stephen J. Krasemann: page 10 (top); Albert Kuhnigk:
    pages 7 (middle), 19 (top); James D. Markou: page 25 (right);
    M. & I. Morcombe: page 21; Karl Weidmann: pages 13, 22

**Illustrations**
Barbara Bedell: pages 6-7, logo on backcover

**Color separations and film**
Dot 'n Line Image Inc.

## Crabtree Publishing Company

350 Fifth Avenue
Suite 3308
New York
N.Y. 10118

360 York Road, RR 4,
Niagara-on-the-Lake,
Ontario, Canada
L0S 1J0

73 Lime Walk
Headington
Oxford OX3 7AD
United Kingdom

**Cataloging in Publication Data**
Kalman, Bobbie
    Rainforest birds

(Birds up close)
Includes index.

ISBN 0-86505-753-2 (library bound)   ISBN 0-86505-767-2 (pbk.)
This book introduces several types of rainforest birds, including parrots,
toucans, and hornbills, and discusses forest-floor dwellers, middle-layer
fliers, and raptors.

1. Rain forest birds—Juvenile literature. [1. Rain forest birds.] I. Title.
II. Series: Kalman, Bobbie. Birds up close.

QL676.2.K3486  1997          j598.1734                    LC 97-39903
                                                          CIP

# Contents

# Birds of the jungle

Thousands of different types of birds live in the wettest, hottest, greenest places on earth—the **tropical rainforests**. Tropical rainforests are places where rain falls almost every day. In order to be called a rainforest, an area must receive more than 80 inches (203 cm) of rain each year, and its tallest trees must be at least 98 feet (30 m) high. The temperature in a tropical rainforest rarely falls below 75°F (24°C). Tropical rainforests are also called **jungles**.

## Where the birds are

Most of the birds in the rainforest live in tree branches high above the ground, where a lot of food can be found. The birds eat insects as well as the fruit, seeds, flowers, and buds that grow on rainforest trees and plants. Many other animals, such as monkeys, frogs, snakes, and lizards, also live in the treetops.

*Sunbirds spend their time flying from flower to flower in search of **nectar**.*

## A habitat in danger

More than half of the millions of plant and animal species on earth are found in the tropical rainforests. About 2,500 of the 9,000 types of birds live in these forests. Even though they are such a rich **habitat**, rainforests cover very little land. They take up less than six percent of all the land on the planet, and they are getting smaller every day. For every acre (0.4 hectare) of rainforest that is cut down, more than 200 species of plants and animals may be lost forever.

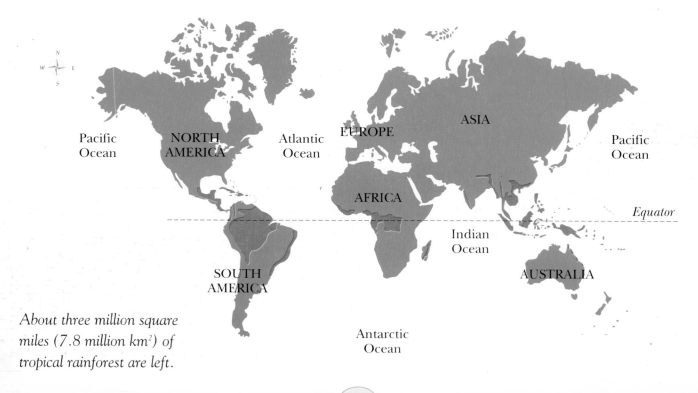

Pacific Ocean

NORTH AMERICA

Atlantic Ocean

EUROPE

ASIA

Pacific Ocean

AFRICA

Equator

Indian Ocean

SOUTH AMERICA

AUSTRALIA

Antarctic Ocean

*About three million square miles (7.8 million km²) of tropical rainforest are left.*

# Three layers

To study rainforests, scientists divide them into three layers—the **forest floor**, the **understory**, and the **canopy**.

## The canopy

The branches and leaves at the top of the tallest trees form a huge, living roof called the canopy. Trees that make up the canopy are between 75 and 150 feet (23-45 m) tall. Giant trees called **emergents** poke through the canopy.

## The understory

The understory begins about 60-70 feet (18-21 m) above the ground. It is made up of small trees, palms, and shrubs. Almost all rainforest birds, animals, and food are found in the understory.

## The forest floor

The forest floor is covered with a thin layer of soil, dead leaves, and fallen trees, branches, and fruit. It is very dark in this part of the rainforest because the leaves and branches of the canopy and understory block most of the sunlight.

canopy

understory

forest floor

Many birds of prey travel between the canopy and the understory to find food. The barn owl pictured on the right is a visitor to the rainforest canopy, where it may nest in a hollow tree.

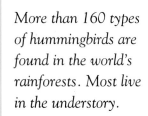

More than 160 types of hummingbirds are found in the world's rainforests. Most live in the understory.

Antbirds live in the lower understory, but they come down to the forest floor to eat ground-dwelling insects. Some types of antbirds catch the insects that run away from long lines of marching army ants.

# On the ground

Birds that live on the forest floor include pheasants, currasows, partridges, and guinea fowl. Jaguars and other large cats are **predators** of these birds. Snakes and rats often prey on their eggs and chicks. Gorillas, hogs, lizards, and frogs also live on the ground, but not all of these animals live in the same rainforests. Birds from other rainforest layers fly down to the ground in search of food and mates.

*Currasows spend the day walking on the ground, but they rest in low trees at night. They have strong toes that help them grip branches.*

## Hiding a nest in plain sight

Eggs and chicks in nests on the ground are easy prey for snakes and other enemies. Many birds build their nest among plants to hide it from predators.

*Some birds, such as this pauraque, hide their eggs with their feathers when they sit on the nest.*

## Eating anything that moves

Most ground-dwelling birds eat foods that are within easy reach of the forest floor. These include fallen fruits and seeds, as well as many insects and worms. Some birds also eat small animals that move along the ground such as lizards and frogs.

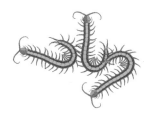

## These birds were made for walking

Many of the birds that live on the rainforest floor are poor fliers. They prefer to walk rather than fly. These birds have strong legs, feet, and claws for walking and for scratching the ground in search of food. They spend most of their time rooting among the fallen leaves and rotten plants to uncover insects and worms.

## Center stage

Several types of birds that live at higher layers of the rainforest come down to the ground when it is time to mate. To attract a female, males gather in a certain area called a **lek** to compete against one another. Each male chooses a low branch or a small part of the forest floor as his stage, where he shows off his bright feathers or performs a **mating dance**.

*(top left) Motmots perch on low branches and watch for prey moving along the ground. They fly down quickly to pounce on small animals such as lizards.*

*(bottom left) Ocellated turkeys are ground dwellers by day, but they spend the night in trees. They make loud noises to keep in contact with one another in the dark parts of the rainforest.*

*(right) The male cock-of-the-rock tries to win a mate by spreading his feathers and tilting his head sideways to show off the large, round crest of feathers on top of his head. He sits very still and watches the female with one eye.*

# Living in the air

The understory is full of life. Most of the rainforest birds and many bats, ocelots, and monkeys live in this layer. Some of these birds and animals never touch the ground! They spend their whole life climbing on tree branches or flying among them.

## Food all around

The birds that live at this layer of the rainforest have little trouble finding food. There are so many types of trees and plants that flowers and fruit grow year round. The millions of insects that live on tree trunks and under the bark are another source of food for birds in the understory.

*(above) Tanagers are songbirds that live mainly in the understory. They also spend a lot of time in the lower part of the canopy. They eat insects and fruit.*

# Sipping flower nectar

Two types of birds are well suited to feeding on the nectar of flowers at all layers of the rainforest, especially those growing in the understory. Hummingbirds have tubelike beaks that reach easily into flowers while the birds hover in front of them. With their long tongue, these birds sip the juices inside flowers. Hummingbirds live in the rainforests of Central and South America.

Sunbirds live in African and Asian rainforests. Like hummingbirds, sunbirds have a thin, tubelike beak and a long tongue for sucking nectar out of flowers. Unlike hummingbirds, sunbirds do not hover to feed on nectar. They have strong toes and claws with which they cling to flowers while they feed.

*Some hummingbirds have a beak that is exactly the right shape to fit inside one or two types of flowers.*

## Fruit eaters

Many of the birds that live in the understory eat fruits such as figs and wild avocados, mangos, and papayas. These birds are an important part of the rainforest habitat. They help spread seeds from the fruit around the forest so that plants will grow in new places. Small seeds pass through a bird's body unharmed. Large seeds drop to the ground after birds eat the fruit growing around them. Fruit-eating birds must eat larger amounts of food each day than birds that eat insects or seeds because fruit is not as nutritious as these other foods.

# Hidden homes

Birds in the understory have to protect themselves from many predators. Larger birds attack them and their young. Snakes and monkeys raid their nests to eat the eggs and chicks. Many understory birds build their nests inside tree holes to hide them from predators. Hornbills in Asia, Africa, and India go to even greater lengths to protect their nest. After the female hornbill lays eggs inside a tree hole high above the ground, she seals the opening with a wall of mud. She remains inside the nest hole until the eggs hatch and her chicks are able to care for themselves.

The male hornbill passes food to the female through a small slit in the mud wall. After a few weeks, bird droppings and bits of uneaten food begin to rot in the nest, and the nest hole becomes a smelly mess. The hornbills put up with the mess, though, because their nest is safe from predators.

*(opposite top) Fruit-eating barbets are picky eaters. They throw away many of the berries they pluck.*

*(opposite bottom) Green pigeons especially enjoy eating figs.*

*(right) Some hornbills follow troops of monkeys through the forest in order to find an easy meal. The monkeys drop pieces of fruit as they eat, and the birds quickly pick them up.*

# Sky-high living

A few rainforest birds, including birds of prey, toucans, macaws, and some hummingbirds, spend most of their time in the leafy canopy. Almost all birds visit more than one layer of the rainforest, however, and many fly freely between the understory and canopy. Most small birds avoid the top of the canopy, though, because they are hunted by the birds of prey, or **raptors**, that live there. Larger birds such as macaws and toucans are almost the same size as the raptors and are difficult to kill.

*Toucans are often called the most noisy and **social** birds in the rainforest. Social birds live and hunt in groups.*

## Big beaks

Toucans are well known for their large, colorful beaks. Some toucans have beaks that are longer than their body! The beak may look solid and heavy, but it is actually hollow inside. Some scientists think the beak's bright colors may scare away enemies.

## Toucan tools

Toucan beaks are very useful. The birds can scrape out a nest hole in a rotten tree trunk with their beak or use it to reach the fruits and berries that grow on the thin tips of branches. These branches would break if the birds climbed on them to pick the fruit.

*Toucans are also called "seed spitters."*
*Most large birds swallow the seeds of the fruit*
*they eat, but toucans spit them out. By spitting*
*seeds around the rainforest, toucans help spread*
*new plants all over the jungle.*

# Mainly raptors

Birds of prey attack and eat almost every type of animal that lives in the jungle, from snakes to sloths. Some raptors fly through the forest to catch prey. Others perch on a branch and watch for animals below them. When they see prey such as a bird or monkey, they swoop down and grab it with their claws. Many rainforest raptors hunt birds that live in the understory or near the ground. A few hunt fish in the rivers and flooded areas of the rainforest.

*Philippine eagles are strong enough to carry large prey such as monkeys. These raptors are also called monkey-eating eagles.*

## Hunters by day or night

Eagles, hawks, and falcons are raptors that hunt in the rainforest during the day. They fly over a large area in search of food. These birds kill their prey where they catch it and then take it to a favorite perch to eat their meal. Owls are **nocturnal** raptors, which means they hunt at night.

*(above) Ornate hawk-eagles build a large nest at the top of one of the tallest trees in their area. They fly down among the lower branches to find prey for their babies.*

*(right) The spectacled owl is a common rainforest raptor. These owls hunt at night and spend the day hiding in tree holes.*

# River and coastal birds

Wide, deep rivers flow through or next to most of the world's large rainforests. Many **wading birds** are found along the edge of these rainforests, near the large bodies of water. Herons and storks are wading birds that walk in the shallow waters in search of food. Other birds such as fish eagles and kingfishers fly over the deeper water to look for fish swimming near the surface.

At certain times of the year, the rivers overflow their banks, creating a large, flooded plain that is full of food for fish-eating birds.

*(opposite) Wading storks such as the yellow-billed stork eat small fish, frogs, crabs, and water insects. Unlike other water birds, they are able to hunt in muddy or murky water because they feel for prey with their beak.*

## Kingfishers

Kingfishers live, eat, and breed along the edge of rivers. They eat large insects, small lizards, fish, and other water animals. When they hunt for fish, they fly close to the surface of the water and dive to catch their prey. Kingfishers grab a fish with their beak, take it to their perch, beat it against the branch, and then swallow it head first. Azure kingfishers, such as the one shown left, live in the Australian rainforest. If they cannot find enough fish to eat, these birds attack flying insects.

# Fine feathers

Many birds have **camouflage** that helps protect them from enemies. Camouflage is a disguise that allows a bird to hide itself even when it is in plain sight. The bird's feathers, or **plumage**, are the same color as the ground, rocks, grass, or trees where it lives. A predator has difficulty spotting a camouflaged bird when it stays completely still in its surroundings.

*A few types of rainforest birds have* **disruptive markings** *such as stripes. Some scientists think that these markings make an animal's body shape difficult for predators to recognize. A striped bird in a tree looks simply like a bunch of branches.*

## A gaudy disguise

A lot of rainforest birds have showy red, blue, and yellow feathers that seem to offer no camouflage at all. Among the green leaves, spotty sunlight, and colorful flowers of the rainforest, however, green plumage with bright patches of color blend in perfectly. A bird sitting quietly on a branch looks like leaves with spots of sunlight shining on them. Even when bright birds fly, their colorful, flapping wings blend in with the splotches of sunlight coming through the canopy.

### Better brown

On the forest floor, very few birds are brightly colored. Most of the birds in this part of the forest have dull brown feathers or dark, speckled plumage. Their dark coloring helps the birds blend into the shady background of the forest floor so that they can hide from predators such as jaguars and other large cats.

# The parrot family

The parrot family is one of the largest families of rainforest birds. It includes hundreds of different species of parrots, parakeets, macaws, lorikeets, lories, rosellas, and cockatoos. These birds come in a rainbow of colors—red, orange, blue, yellow, and green. Most rainforest parrots live their whole life in the canopy and understory. They spend most of their time in the trees, where they eat, climb, shriek, squawk, and play.

*Rainbow lorikeets love to eat pollen, nectar, fruit, berries, and seeds. They hang upside-down from branches to reach the nectar and pollen in flowers.*

## Great giants

Macaws, shown right, are the longest and brightest birds in the parrot family. They are easy to recognize because of the large, bare patches of skin that ring their eyes. Their plumage is bright red and green or blue and gold.

People have always hunted macaws for their beautiful feathers. Trappers sometimes put a sticky substance on branches to catch adult macaws when they perch. Most hunters climb trees and take the chicks from their nest holes.

*Salmon-crested cockatoos raise their bright crest when they are excited or curious.*

## All in the family

Parrots come in many sizes and colors, but they all have two body parts that are similar—their bill and their feet. They can use their beak to do delicate jobs such as **preening**, or combing their feathers, but the bill is also strong enough to crush the hardest nuts. It often serves as a third "foot." When parrots climb, they use it as a hook to pull themselves up and down branches.

Parrots' feet are unusual. Most birds have three toes that point forward and one that points backward. On a parrot's feet, two toes point backward and two point forward. This arrangement gives parrots a strong grip for climbing trees. Parrots can also use their feet like hands, as shown on page 25. With one foot, a parrot picks up and moves objects close to its bill.

*Rose-ringed parakeets are not afraid of people. They often live near cities and farms.*

## Left or right?

Most parrots are left- or right-footed, just as people are left- or right-handed. When parrots eat, they balance on one foot and use their **dominant**, or preferred, foot to hold the food. They also use their dominant foot to scratch their head.

## Hanging around

A parrot's feet are so strong that the bird can use them to hang upside-down from branches. One type of parrot even hangs upside-down to sleep, just as bats do. This type of parrot is known as the hanging parakeet. To reach for food, parrots often use their strong grip to perch sideways, as shown right.

## More about parrots

**Number of Species:** 330
**Length:** 3 - 40 inches (8 - 102 cm)
**Weight:** 4 ounces - 8 pounds (0.1 - 3.6 kg)
**Food:** Vegetables, fruit, seeds, and flowers
**Predators:** Snakes, hawks; also wildcats when they can catch them

# Caged birds

Trapping birds for sale is a big business. Every year, more than 20 million birds are traded around the world. Some are **endangered**, which means they are in danger of disappearing forever.

Catching and selling endangered birds is against the law, but trappers do so anyway because people pay thousands of dollars for an unusual or rare rainforest bird. Until people stop buying these threatened birds, trappers will continue to capture them. Many of these birds could soon be **extinct**, or gone forever.

## Too many die

More than ten captured birds die for each one that becomes a pet. Some are killed by accident when they are caught, and others die while being moved to other countries. The birds are tied up and shipped in small containers. Some suffocate. Others die because they are not given enough food and water for the trip.

*Some people think it is impressive to have an endangered harpy eagle chained in their yard. What do you think?*

# Bred in captivity

If you are thinking of buying one of these birds, make sure that it is **bred in captivity**. Birds bred in captivity are not taken from the wild. They are hatched and raised by people called **breeders**.

Some breeders also raise rare birds to try to save them from extinction. These people raise chicks and train them to live on their own in the wild. They often release adult birds into a nature preserve or park, where people cannot hunt them.

*These rare parrots are waiting to be released into the wild as part of a captive breeding program.*

# Losing their home

Rainforests are the most endangered habitats in the world. Every year, people cut down huge areas of these forests. Trees are cut for lumber and to clear ground for farms, cities, roads, and mines. When the trees are cut down, the remaining plants in the rainforest soon die, creating a large wasteland. Cutting down the rainforest may even change the weather by speeding up **global warming**. Trees take carbon dioxide and other "greenhouse gases" from the air. Fewer trees means more of these gases are in the air, trapping heat from the sun and causing global warming.

*People cut down the rainforest to grow grass for cattle. Farm crops raised on cleared rainforest land include coffee and bananas.*

## Birds without homes

When a rainforest is cut down, all the animals and birds living in it lose their homes, and they often become endangered. For example, the monkey-eating eagle of Asia is now near extinction because the rainforest where it lives is getting smaller every day. This bird of prey needs to hunt in a large area in order to find enough food. The thousands of birds that migrate every year from North America to the South American rainforests will lose their winter homes if these rainforests continue to disappear.

*Quetzals and other tree-hole nesters need hollow trees in which to build their nest. When the rainforest is logged, fewer older trees with suitable holes are left for these birds.*

# Words to know

**canopy** The top layer of the rainforest, made up of the tops of the tallest trees

**dominant** Describing something that has control or is most important

**endangered** Describing a type of plant or animal that is in danger of dying out

**extinction** The state of a type of plant or animal that has died out

**forest floor** The ground level of a jungle

**global warming** The slow rise in world temperatures, caused in part by air pollution

**habitat** The place where a plant or animal is usually found in nature

**hover** To stay in one place in the air

**mating dance** A set of movements that an animal performs to attract a partner for breeding

**nectar** A sweet liquid found inside many flowers

**plumage** A bird's feathers

**predator** An animal that kills and eats other animals

**raptor** A bird of prey that catches prey with its feet and claws

**understory** The middle layer of a rainforest, made up of palms, ferns, and small trees

**wading bird** A bird that walks in shallow water to find most of its food

# Index

1 2 3 4 5 6 7 8 9 0   Printed in the U.S.A.   6 5 4 3 2 1 0 9 8 7